The Peculiar
Lord Timothy Dexter

Includes Bonus Book--A Pickle for the Knowing Ones

By

Stefan James Madison

LAKE FOREST
PUBLISHING

TABLE OF CONTENTS

INTRODUCTION

Lord Timothy Dexter was seen as a fortunate cynic for exporting coal to Newcastle and bed warmers to the tropical areas while still somehow managing to earn a profit. He collected stray cats in federalist Newburyport, Massachusetts, and sent them to the Caribbean. He authored a novel that was semiliterate but lacked grammar, and it went through eight re-prints.

He was a well-known 18th-century businessman who engaged in a succession of rash dealings and was paid richly each time. He was a humble, illiterate leatherworker who became one of Boston's wealthiest men by continuously and naively betting on the Continental dollar and persistently campaigning for entrance into the sophisticated professional network for decades.

Timothy Dexter did fail at the one thing that really mattered to him: high-class acceptability. Maybe it was due to the fact that he was indubitably pretentious and obnoxious.

After all, he did refer to himself as a lord, arranged his own fake burial, and surrounded his High Street house with carved wooden sculptures of historical figures. But the question remains: was he extraordinarily fortunate or extraordinarily clever?

This book is about the great personality of Lord Timothy Dexter, who became successful quickly and was given the title of Lord. Keep reading this book to know more about Lord Timothy Dexter and his life. I have also included his book, *"A Pickle for the Knowing Ones"* in the back of this book for you to reference at your leisure.

CHAPTER I

His Childhood And Early Life

Timothy Dexter was born on January 22, 1747 in Malden, Massachusetts, which lies a few miles outside of Boston. A century previously, the first Dexter had arrived in America from Ireland. Timothy's family was very poor, and this led him to being minimally educated as a child. Though, he envisioned himself as a legendary person from the moment he was born — "I was going to be one great [sic] man," he later claimed — although fate was not on his side.

He belonged to a family of agricultural laborers who had little financial security during the British colonial period. At a very young age, namely eight, he began working without pay on his family's farmland. He left the farmland at 14 to train as an assistant, preparing leather for breeches and gloves in Charlestown, Massachusetts. Dexter was able to gain an apprenticeship with a Boston leather designer by the age of 16 and started working towards a craftsman career from that point on. The firm manager presented him with a new suit, which he aptly called the "freedom suit" after he completed his training.

Although the job was deemed "lower class", the pay was good; as, by the 1760s, Dexter's Boston professors had monopolized the skill of making "Moroccan leather", a material in limited supply and high demand among colonial trendsetters.

Dexter finished his training at 21 and started his own company, within such he made leather gloves and moosehide breeches. Although the situation in Boston soon deteriorated—the British enforced "taxation without representation," citizens protested with the Boston Tea Party, and the government blocked the city's ports—Dexter remained in the city.

In time he decided his best option would be to go to Charlestown, Boston's leatherette hub, equipped only with a "bindle" (hobo-stick) slung over his shoulders.

Meeting his Wife

Dexter sold his freedom suit for 8 dollars and twenty cents, which helped to finance his transfer to Newburyport in 1767. Many artists and tradespeople moved to the seaside town during the time. Newburyport's economy grew to the point that it was second only to Boston in terms of commercial prominence. To put this more in perspective: Shipbuilders in Newburyport produced 70 boats in the year 1767 alone.

Here Dexter encountered (and seduced) Elizabeth Frothingham, the rich, newly minted widow of one of his old leather colleagues, through his first stroke of luck. She was a hardworking, thrifty lady who had made "no inconsiderable profit" selling door-to-door items as a hawker. Dexter took her hand in marriage within a year, less enamored with her nature than with her financial value. She was already the mother of four children and the owner of a home, as she was a striking nine years older than him. He established a business in his wife's cellar, retailing moosehide pants, gloves, skins, and fat. Elizabeth also started a novelties store around this time.

Dexter's life was a roller coaster full of astounding highs and painful lows. With the end of the American Revolution, he accumulated many thousand dollars, only to later squander it all on worthless Continental money. Fortunately for him, his luck was persistent - Congress eventually chose to honor the very same notes that he had wasted his fortune on, overnight making him a very wealthy man. Was this merely a stroke of luck or did he possess an uncanny foresight? Whatever it may be, we can't help but admire his remarkable journey and celebrate his success.

CHAPTER 2

His Professional Life

His Increase in Wealth by Chance

Dexter was an immediate outcast in Boston's affluent Charlestown area. His new neighbors, including John Hancock (the then-Governor of the Commonwealth) and Thomas Russel (one of the state's wealthiest men), were America's aristocracy, well-versed in decorum and commercial dealings. Dexter was not treated equally due to the fact that he was an ignorant, "lowly" guy who had married into wealth rather than earning it on his own front. This only enraged him, which inspired him to go out to demonstrate his decency.

Dexter started by getting a position in public service after seeing his gentlemen counterparts. He submitted scores of petitions to the adjacent Malden, the MA governmental body, in hopes he could serve. Proficiency was not on his side as he was a person who had dropped out of school at eight years old, until (most probably out of weariness) they eventually established a position for him entitled: "Informer of Deer." Dexter was assigned keeping track of the town's fawn numbers, although, according to the chronicles of Malden's government archives, "The last deer had gone from the Malden woods nineteen years ago."

Dexter was content with his new responsibilities, and thus he set out to increase his fortune. And of course in typical Dexterian fashion, he came up with an unusual way to accomplish his objectives.

Dexter and the Congress

The Continental Congress (formed by the thirteen colonies to oppose British authority) produced America's initial form of paper currency, the Continental dollar, which varied in value from 16 cents to $80 at the start of the Revolutionary War in 1775. Despite several attempts by Congress to penalize non-participating shop keepers and owners, the currency's value was greatly weakened––even during the Revolution itself. Although Congress issued $250 million worth of notes, merchants refused to take them because they did not believe in the currency's value.

The story of Timothy Dexter's success is an inspiring tale of humble beginnings that end in triumph. After years of hard work and dedication, he finally achieved wealth and renown in 1791 or 1792 - what could be considered a Cinderella story. According to John P. Marquand, an American writer of that period, this newfound wealth allowed Dexter to slip away from the life of nonstop labor he had grown accustomed to; instead, the remarkable Timothy Dexter of mythology and tradition was born. Even though his success was relatively fast-tracking compared to his previous decades of laboriousness, it was still refreshingly heartwarming – he had been rewarded for his diligence with substantial riches.

Congress was ultimately obliged to issue more banknotes, which quickly swamped the marketplace and depreciated in worth. The expression, "not worth a Continental," had been used at the time to describe a product's complete lack of appreciation. Soldiers who were compensated in Continentals were penniless after the war, and Dexter's wealthy neighbors,

Hancock and Russel, purchased back a few of these notes "to bolster people's confidence and do a charitable act."

Dexter, who was always watching from the shadows and craving respect, tried to imitate these individuals plus some. He pooled all of his funds (along with his wife's) and acquired boatloads of the notes for fractions of a penny on the dollar, realizing that Americans were eager to part with the now-discontinued Continentals for basically anything that they could get. It was a risky and foolish decision since he was betting his entire livelihood on reintroducing this money, with little prospect of profit.

Though his risk paid off, thanks to a wonderful stroke of luck. The Constitution of The United States provided that the Continentals may be exchanged for government bonds at 1% of surface-level when the decision was approved in the 1790s, primarily at Alexander Hamilton's request. Dexter grew immediately and substantially wealthy after purchasing large amounts of this money at a fraction of the cost.

Dexter had also acquired significant numbers of European currencies (British pounds and French francs) on the dubious advice of a neighbor who had developed a dislike to him, which he could now sell for a good profit. Dexter reasoned; his new money would help him acquire respect among his colleagues. This, however, was not the case. Dexter's attempts to enter into the upper crust's intellectual circles were often thwarted by his "crude" speech, unpleasant personality, and inability to keep his lips closed at inappropriate times.

After two long decades of living in the large city of Boston and facing rejection from his peers, John felt it was time to make a change. Taking his wife and family with him, he set off for the town of Newburyport. The seaside setting seemed to have a calming effect on John—instead of retreating into himself and feeling like an outcast, he experienced a newfound sense of belonging. With increased confidence and passion, he was able to begin a fresh chapter. It was truly heartwarming to see him blossom among the casual yet warm atmosphere of Newburyport.

Newburyport

Newburyport was a reportedly ideal town during the late 1700s, with there being a great handful of "rich and poor mingling" as well as the "population not [being] so big as to hide any individual, however strange or modest." Timothy Dexter wasted no time in seizing the opportunity presented by his presence.

He spent his newfound wealth on a thriving fleet of ships, a stable of bright cream-colored horses, and an opulent carriage emblazoned with his initials. Then, in grand style, he built a "princely chateau" which overlooked the sea—complete with the most opulent furniture available, even down to the most "delightful and commodious outhouses."

According to a 19th-century scholar, Dexter then commissioned the most brilliant and tasteful European architects to sculpt and install a series of over 40 massive wooden sculptures on his land, each portraying a legendary figure from American history. I will write greater detail of the statues in chapter 3 but will touch on it briefly now.

He had the last statue be of himself, so as not to be outdone. The 40 sculptures, priced at around $2,000 each, cost Dexter twice as much as his whole estate — but they helped him achieve his ultimate goal: attracting public attention. Samuel L. Knapp said, "It made the simpletons stare, and it brought the owners the greatest joy."

Though unfortunately for him, Dexter began to attract the wrong type of attention. His estate had become such an eyesore that his wife moved out to live somewhere else in the neighborhood; in her absence, Dexter's son — a glum young man who, like his father, had little interest in learning — moved in. The house was quickly transformed into a "bagnio" (brothel) of sorts, with long evenings of drunken buffoonery, ladies coming and going, and the exquisite furnishings (including drapes owned by the Queen of France) being covered with "unseemly stains, unpleasant to sight and smell."

In the neighborhood, Dexter was making a giant fool of himself. Everyone looked on with a deep sorrow, although this disappointment was quickly replaced by bemusement at his poor choices. You could probably see it in their eyes, they all felt sorry for him. Sadly, he only seemed to grow more reckless and absurd as time went on. Although his foolishness was entertaining at first, the longer it lasted the less humorous it became causing most to feel pity rather than laughter.

Bed Warmers and Cats

He purchased Nathaniel Tracy's beautiful home on State Street, which today houses the Newburyport Public Library. The Congress and the Mehitabel were the names of the two major ships which he constructed. The odd — yet fortunate — transactions he made are still remembered to this day.

Despite the local protests heating up, he decided to stay dedicated to his work and aim for a greater good. Carrying coal to Newcastle for sale at a profit, in addition to sending bed warmers items to the West Indies for profit where they were used as equipment at a molasses company was truly remarkable.

When faced with the difficult decision of what to do with the stray cats in Newburyport, voters managed a 50-50 split on whether or not to have them killed. Fortunately, Dexter had an even better solution. He placed an advertisement in the newspaper offering to pay for all the cats, and he promptly shipped them off to the Caribbean. Through some stroke of luck, they happened to arrive in an area where needed farmers wanted mousers to tackle a mouse infestation afflicting their crops. It was truly heartwarming that Dexter was able to find good homes for all of these cats and make sure that they were taken care of properly.

Dexter's ambition and resourcefulness was extraordinary, as he not only created a successful business in the whalebone market but also branched out and shipped mittens to Polynesia. These were popular with Portuguese merchants who frequently traveled through China on their routes, proving just how far Dexter's reach extended. It is heartwarming to imagine him, a regular person contributing something unique to the world. Although his accounts may have been exaggerated by him, Dexter should be celebrated for his entrepreneurial spirit and drive that made his products available to large cities around the world.

There's Were Some Personal Problems at Home.

Timothy Dexter's economic success did not translate to his personal life as his life at home was far from rosy. His irritable wife chastised him frequently but was not without reason. He had a bad temper and drank excessively.

Elizabeth Dexter undoubtedly aided his yearning for approval. She was descended from the Gilman dynasty of New Hampshire, which had provided a governor to the state, John Taylor Gilman. Timothy Dexter had dealt with his wife's family in property investment, and they undoubtedly looked down upon him. In his own insecurity, he started calling her a ghost and refused to believe she was still alive.

Samuel and Nancy were their two children. Samuel, at least Dexter believed, would grow up to be a well-educated nobleman. Though instead he became a belligerent alcoholic. Sam persuaded his parents to allow him to sell cargo aboard one of his ships in England. Rather, he squandered it all in the gambling arena.

Nancy was attractive, but she lacked intelligence like her father. She married a Yale academic with little wealth, Abraham Bishop, and relocated to New Haven with him immediately following their wedding. The relationship ended in divorce, as he abused her both physically and mentally, which caused her to start drinking frequently. Nancy came home in time, where her family locked her up because they knew fully well that alcohol did not help her already poor wits.

It is heartbreaking to see individuals burdened with the challenges that come with destructive habits and lifestyles handed down through generations. In Dexter's case, it seems he may have been looking for a better way - unfortunately, his path ran out before he could steer towards a more positive destination. We can only imagine what could have been if Dexter was able to discover a healthier lifestyle sooner and if his children were able to receive its benefits in the formative years of their lives. The prospect of greater possibilities for him and those closest to him lingers in our collective minds, but for now, we'll never truly know what might have been.

Dexter's poverty-stricken plight had caused him great anxiety. With a heart full of hope and a head full of worries, he sold his beloved Tracy home and moved to Chester, New Hampshire in 1796.

The Ingenious Eccentric

I want to share a bit more detail on Dexter's investments as it is truly remarkable. When Dexter bought several big ships and declared his plans to start a firm in international commerce, his enraged neighbors allegedly jumped at the chance to present him with bad investment opportunities—forcing him to relocate.

One neighbor suggested Dexter sell warm pots in the West Indies (large, flat metal pans with large handles in use for warming beddings in the 18th century) (a European colonial area also famous for the year-round warm weather). Dexter, ever trusting, acquired 42,000 pans, spread them among nine cargo boats, and went out to sell them, all the while drawing loud laughter from seasoned merchants. Though of course Dexter got the last laugh: when he arrived and saw that the warming devices were no longer needed, he marketed them as ladles and resold them to molasses and sugar factory owners.

The market was so high that every owner insisted on purchasing at minimum three or four pans; Dexter grossly overpriced the pans, by 79 percent, and came back with even more money than he'd started with.

In another case, a dealer deceived Dexter into believing that raw coal was in a growing market in Newcastle. Unseen to Dexter, the area already had a big coal mine, making any foreign cargo worthless. By chance, the mine was mysteriously on strike when Dexter approached, and the coal was acquired at a significant mark-up. Dexter triumphed once more, this time with "one [gallon] and a quarter of silver."

By this time, Dexter had amassed a substantial understanding of trading tactics because of his experiences. At least one 19th-century chronicler claims that from this moment onwards, Dexter's activities were "very sane" marketing ploys to deceive his critics, rather than acts of idiocy or ignorance. As his money grew, he realized that he could simply ask whatever product was scarce in the market, buy as much as he could, then double the price and sell it.

He employed this technique with elegance, even though his commodities of choice were frequently bizarre.

Dexter allegedly scurried once to Boston and acquired an enormous amount of whales bones — so much so he was able to control the marketplace for the item and set his personal price rate. He accumulated 340 tons of whale bones, which he sold at a 75 percent profit for use in items such as women's corsets, collar stays, buggy whips, toys, and even machines. Whalebone and baleen were in such a growing market they are now referred to as the plastics of the 19th century.

Dexter, on the other hand, wasn't beyond employing shady tactics to market his products. He allegedly boasted about buying wholesale Bibles for "12 percent under half price," or 41 cents per piece, and then manipulating the sale of 21,000 units in the West Indies. He added, with little concern for spelling, that he sent a message that there should be a Bible in every family home, or they must go through Hell themselves. He then assured his potential customers that his commanders would be ready with a full supply if they wanted to repent and go to paradise. Dexter had swept $47,000 worth of sacred texts in only a few weeks.

Timothy Dexter's journey of selling books with holy words has stirred the hearts of many around the world. Despite his questionable intentions of just setting up a business, it was much more than that - he was unknowingly bringing hope and morality to faraway places. His efforts have been like a comforting light in the dark, providing people with faith in times of despair. Through Dexter's actions, it is evident how God works in mysterious ways.

The Earl of Chester.

Though it may be hard to believe, Dexter had an unbelievable business drive and dedication to work. Despite his well-known issue with alcohol, he had the fortitude to separate work from pleasure - something that surely required vigilance and commitment. Irving Wallace famously quipped that "Timothy Dexter's fortune was built on discipline and a hangover", pointing out that though he occasionally partied in the evenings, come day, he stayed sober and stayed focused on his business dealings.

CHAPTER 3

How He Was Named As "Lord Timothy Dexter"

Dexter had positioned himself as the distinguishing eccentric of Newburyport, Massachusetts, and the Eastern regions at the end of the eighteenth century. Despite his belief that there is no such thing as "bad" attention, rumors of his wealth and antics spread far beyond his seaside village.

More than ever, he wished to be recognized as a noble, affluent gentleman, but his actions created a barrier between him and the people he admired. Dexter reeked of bad taste and lack of knowledge to gentry men, and the man's actions confirmed their fears.

Dexter would frequently have the labels on his sculptures repainted (as he enjoyed rewriting history on occasion). When an unlucky painter scribbled "Declaration of Independence" beneath a monument of Thomas Jefferson, Dexter insisted that he change it to "Constitution" (a wrong attribution). When the artist insisted on using his own inscription, Dexter took out his long-rifle and fired shots at him, missing by a hair. With a serious tone, he repeated, "Constitution." His painter simply complied this time.

Lord Dexter returned to Newburyport after his attack and purchased a magnificent estate held by Nathaniel Tracy's business associate, Jonathan Jackson.

On the grounds, he built an exterior museum with 40 beautifully decorated wooden sculptures of Louis XVI, Adam and Eve, Toussaint Louverture, and John Hancock. The initial three presidents of the United States sat atop a massive arch. Additionally, Dexter had at least one monument with the inscription, "I am the first one in the East, the first one in the West, and the brightest philosopher in the Western World."

Dexter's creative craziness was anything but senseless. Marquand came to recognize that his unique plan of creating an 'external museum' by the Essex-Merrimack bridge was more successful than anticipated - giving traffic from across the bridge a surge of new customers and bringing some laughs to the area. There were many fascinating stories surrounding the building, not least of which were about the attractive young damsels who frequented it and with whom Dexter engaged in improper behavior.

It was crazy to see the lengths this gentleman would go to try and emulate his neighbors. Although he never stayed to read beyond ten minutes as he personally struggled in that area, his efforts were not in vain. Upon hearing of the English nobility's love for works of art, he felt moved and decided that he should have his own collection too. He hired a servant so dedicated that he was willing to work day and night until the gallery was complete.

Dexter associated himself with its most eccentric, off-beat personalities he could find, possibly the only people ready to accompany him to get respect from the wealthy elite. Lord Dexter sought acclaim and solace from misanthropes and sycophants as his drinking addiction further deteriorated. One person was John, a gentleman from a respected family who had been an outcast after being dismissed as a schoolteacher and starting his own institution. He was a person of permanent paradoxes, who patiently taught "scientific" information to students who had no prior understanding or training in the field. He rapidly became Dexter's best buddy and motivator. Madam Hooper, a wealthy widow-turned-fortune-teller who, among other things, provided Dexter astrological guidance in return for tea, struck up a similar connection with him. To elaborate, Madame Hooper had a rooster for a friend and had a double set of teeth. Jonathan Plummer, a fisherman, wrote poems praising Dexter's grandeur. He also had a small dog, most likely a Mexican hairless, who stayed by his side even when he was drinking––unlike his wife and kids.

Dexter famously recruited his own poet laureate, a hapless 20-year-old he'd spotted in the market peddling halibut from a wheelbarrow in imitation of the King of England. Dexter fashioned a coronet of parsley (the only item he had in his garden at the time) and compelled his new lyricist to compose and perform adoring poetry that enhanced his self-esteem after discovering that the great Italian poets were crowned with mistletoe. Despite this, Dexter's craving for adoration was not satisfied by the poetry. He'd frequently wander the streets of nearby cities, stopping passers-by from inquiring about "the greatest man in the East." Dexter would then tell his own fantastical, self-gratifying story regardless of his victim's reaction.

He soon called himself "Lord", insisting that his guardsmen, servants, and crew members address him as such. They were so used to his pranks that they asked no more questions: he was dubbed "Lord Timothy Dexter".

But Dexter was no fool: despite the forced adoration, he saw that his colleagues didn't appreciate him, which troubled him immensely. Dexter planned to fake his own death in a fit of desperation. He intended to have a better understanding of how the general people felt about him by doing so.

Dexter's Death Prank.

His arrangements began with a coffin, which took up the whole cellar of a magnificent summer home and was extravagant and well-ventilated. The trickster then engaged Massachusetts' greatest cabinetmaker to create a coffin out of the finest mahogany wood available — so beautiful that once it was finished, Dexter slept in it for many weeks with great pleasure and delight.

With the mechanics of his test in place, Dexter engaged the services of a handful of his trusted men to stage a pretend funeral and to distribute tiny cards informing the town of his death. His wife and two kids were told about the deception, and he ordered that they take their specific roles and act out by crying and acting devastated.

Approximately 3,000 individuals attended the ceremony on the day of the event. Dexter gleefully viewed the spectacle from behind a wall of wooden boards, where only the finest wines and most unusual liquors were poured. His son was "sufficiently inebriated to weep without any effort," while his daughter's head was covered in her hands. Dexter was startled when he saw his tear-free, smiling wife.

He confronted her in the kitchen in stealth, then savagely struck her for her lack of ambition, making a disturbance. The deceased Dexter, who now had an ear-to-ear smile, welcomed the other guests as they walked into the room. The exposed red-handed fool then went about partying with his buddies as if the whole thing had never occurred. When all the townspeople discovered his plot, it must have been a surreal scene to witness. Everyone must've felt surprised, confused and scared all at once. In that moment, I wish I could've been a fly on the wall - to observe the reaction.

Writing the Book - A Pickle for the Knowing Ones.

Lord Timothy Dexter was a man with a single goal - the desire to be remembered for eternity. To accomplish this immense aspiration, he followed in the footsteps of great leaders from history before him and wrote his own memoir. Dexter's pursuit of everlasting recognition through his book did get him remembered that is for sure but for different reasons.

Despite his utter lack of expertise (or interest) in reading and handwriting, he set out to write a book that would outsmart Shakespeare and challenge Milton's learning. "A Pickle for the Knowing Ones, or Plain Truths in a Homespun Dress," was his marketing slogan (which made absolutely no sense). The book was horribly misspelt and lacking of any punctuation — no periods, commas, dashes, or hyphens — and was simply a confused tangle of virtually unintelligible language.

Dexter wrote the 24-page booklet in 1802, in which he was critical of the clergy, politics, and his spouse. He gave the book away for free, but it became so popular that it had to be re-printed eight times. Dexter included a page containing 13 lines of punctuation marks and directions for readers to distribute how they liked in the second version. Wallace considered it an arrogant, prejudiced, harsh justification of Dexter, by Dexter, against all "Enemies" who were considered to be against him.

Though Dexter's language faults were most likely due to his lack of education, he most likely exaggerated them to ridicule people who dismissed him. According to literary historian Paul Collins, "He had a mistrust of anyone with a college degree, and he loved to rub their nose in it. He would say, 'I have the cash to distribute books as well, and I can do anything I want.'" He truly was the talk of the town.

Dexter noticed that most noblemen in England didn't sell their own books, preferring to give them out as presents to promote reading, so he did the same, standing by the highway and handing out copies to passers-by. His opus gained acclaim over time, if not for its merits, then for its uniqueness. A second version was issued due to great demand. Like I mentioned before, Dexter inserted a whole page of punctuation points at the ending of the book this time, at the request of his publisher, with a clear message for the reader: "salt and pepper them as you wish." Dexter continued to get tremendous, if not semi-satirical, appreciation for his efforts even a century later. His luck strikes again even years after his death!

CHAPTER 4

His Death And Afterwards

Dexter planned his fake funeral just before his death, persuading his family to go through with the lie. He was curious to see how others would respond. After which, he beat his wife senselessly since she didn't weep sufficiently.

On October 26, 1806, Lord Timothy Dexter passed away at the early age of 59, leaving much cash for the needy of Newburyport. The statues at his estate were destroyed in the 1815 hurricane, and they were auctioned for only a few dollars. Those that didn't sell were set ablaze.

Lord Timothy Dexter's life was a wild and unique one. He seemed to go through many extreme highs and lows as he experienced different cultures around the world, but he managed to survive his sometimes reckless adventures during this journey. He even went so far as to remark that being a Lord was a difficult situation to work while on his travels. He took unimaginable risks during this time, drank excessive amounts of alcohol, and contracted several diseases- yet he never backed away from situations that seemed too dangerous or chaotic for most people in his social circle. Lord Dexter was remembered as an unusual figure with a legacy of fleeting moments that were not ultimately forgotten.

Dexter attempted to make amends for his mistakes in his final days by distributing his wealth equally to his children, wife, and friends, leaving no one disappointed.

His desire to be placed in the same coffin he'd created years ago was denied by the Newburyport Board of Health because it was seen as unhygienic. Nevertheless, the Lord was buried in a small hillside cemetery, where wheatgrass soon covered his tombstone.

The Timothy Dexter home was converted into a bar and later passed through several hands. John P. Marquand observed that it was home to numerous rich families who added Victorian touches and that it was difficult to determine where Dexter ended and the Victorians began.

Artists set it ablaze in 1988 by stripping paintwork with a torch. The dome and golden eagle on the rooftop were lost in the fire, but the Society kept the original plans for the Preservation of New England Architecture (currently Historic New England). The home was reconstructed and is held by a private organization.

In her book, Reminiscences of a Newburyport Nonagenarian, Sarah Anna Emery recalled Dexter, written years after his death. She claimed that though uneducated and illiterate, and likely partly owing to his good fortune to success, it is clear that Lord Timothy Dexter was both smart and eloquent, making him a lucky person.

Current Thoughts About Lord Timothy Dexter

Today, those familiar with Lord Dexter have mixed feelings about him: some call him weird and stupid, while others praise him as a genius. Author Francis Drake describes Dexter as a guy who "lacked that type of caution which so frequently masks evil and sets off excellent characteristics," in the Dictionary of American Biography, which is a compilation of notable persons.

Nonetheless, there seemed to be something respectable in Dexter's complete contempt for normalcy: despite his constant attempts to gain recognition from the upper class, he never stopped doing things his own peculiar way.

Lord Dexter was an extraordinary individual, notable for his willingness to flout the rules. He had a complete disregard for conventions and established principles — habits that earned him both admiration and disdain from those he encountered. He made it his mission to carve out a unique path in life, following no one else but himself. His strong convictions undoubtedly drew both detractors and believers alike, making Lord Dexter's life story unlike any other!

CONCLUSION

This book has been about the historical figure Lord Timothy Dexter, who used his good fortune and luck to become rich and famous. Most notably, Lord Dexter was one of America's earliest well-known misanthropes, although he is mostly overlooked in history. This is a pure tragedy.

Lord Dexter was a unique individual who opted to remain peculiar despite his efforts to be liked by others. His journey as a self-made man gives hope and inspiration for those who may start with little but can achieve great success given the right circumstances. Though he made questionable decisions, we too can reap the benefits of his story by learning from his missteps and striving to create a better future for our own family and the generations that follow. He has left behind an example of courage, perseverance, and determination that should be honored for years to come.

A PICKLE FOR THE KNOWING ONES,

BY LORD TIMOTHY DEXTER,

WITH AN

Introductory Preface,

BY A DISTINGUISHED CITIZEN OF "OULD NEWBERRY."

FOURTH EDITION.

NEWBURYPORT:

BLANCHARD & SARGENT.

1848.

Lord Dexter and his Dog.

PREFACE.

Timothy Dexter, the author of the following curious and unique production, entitled *"A Pickle for the Knowing Ones,"* which is here re-printed verbatim et spellatim from the original edition, was born in Malden, January 22, 1747. Having served an apprenticeship with a leather dresser, he commenced business in Newburyport shortly after he was one and twenty, and being industrious and economical, he soon found himself in good circumstances. In the year 1770 he married, and receiving a considerable amount of money with his wife, he was thus put in possession of a moderate fortune. In 1776 he had for one of his apprentices the no less eccentric, and afterwards the no less noted Jonathan Plumer, jun., "travelling preacher, physician and poet," as he was accustomed to style himself, and of whom we shall hereafter speak. In addition to his regular business of selling leather breeches, gloves "soutabel for wimen's ware," &c. he engaged in commercial speculations, and in various kinds of business, and was unusually successful. He traded with merchants and speculators in the then Province of Maine, was engaged to some extent in the West India trade. He also purchased a large amount of what were called State securities, which were eventually redeemed at prices far exceeding their original cost. Some of his speculations in whalebone and warming pans are mentioned by himself on page 23 of this work. Thus in various ways he added to his property, and in a few years he became a wealthy man. With wealth came the desire of distinction, and as his vanity was inordinate he spared no expence in obtaining the notoriety he sought. In the first place he purchased an elegant house in High Street, Newburyport, and embellished it in his peculiar way. Minarets surmounted with golden balls were placed on the roof, a large gilt eagle was placed on the top, and a great variety of other ornaments. In front of his house and land he caused to be erected between forty and fifty wooden statues, full length and larger than life. The principal arch stood directly in front of his door, and on this stood the figures of Washington, Adams and Jefferson. There were also the statues of William Pitt, Franklin, Bonaparte, George IV, Lord Nelson, Gen. Morgan, Cornplanter, an Indian Chief, Jack Tar, Traveling Preacher, Maternal Affection, Two Grenadiers, Four Lions and one Lamb, and conspicuous among them were two images of Dexter himself, one of which held a label with the inscription "*I am the first in the East, the first in the West, and the greatest philosopher in the Western world.*" In order that the interior of his house should correspond with the exterior, the most costly furniture was imported from France, and the walls hung with paintings, brought from Holland and other parts of Europe. A library was also provided, but how large or valuable we are not able to say. An elegant coach with a span of beautiful cream colored horses was procured, on which was painted his coat of arms, with the baronial supporters, after the manner of the English nobility. With this equipage he took the title of Lord Dexter, because, as he said, it was "the voice of the people at Large." He was sometimes called the Marquis of Newburyport. Having completed the embelishments of his house and gardens, Lord Dexter busied himself in receiving the visits of the crowds, who were drawn by curiosity to his house. His gardens were thrown open to their inspection, and he was liberal to all. The fame of his hospitality attracted as many visitors as the fame of his images. To gratify his vanity he selected in imitation of European princes, a poet laureate. This was no other than his former apprentice, Jonathan Plumer, jun., a native of Newbury. [4] They had once been associated as master and apprentice, but now stood in the relation of patron and poet. From the auto-biography of Plumer a very curious and scarce production of 244 pages, the following extract is taken, which may serve to give some idea of the versatility of his genius.—"I had," says he, "some practice as a physician, and earned something with my pen, but for several years was obliged chiefly to follow various kinds of business accounted less honorable, viz: Farming, repeating select passages from authors, selling halibut, sawing wood, selling books and ballads in the streets, serving as post boy, filling beds with straw and wheeling them to the owners thereof, collecting rags, &c." He had previously served one or two campaigns as a soldier, and on his return from the wars he taught school for some time in New Hampshire. The ballads, which he hawked about, were generally his own composition. Every horrid accident, bloody murder, a shipwreck, or any other dreadful catastrophe, was sure to be followed by a statement of the facts, a sermon and a poem. In the capacity of ballad maker and monger he attracted the notice of Dexter, in whose service he entered for a small salary as poet laureate. He wore a livery, consisting of a black frock coat, adorned with stars and fringes, a cocked hat and black breeches. He was crowned in the garden of his patron with a wreath of parsley, instead of laurel, but the ceremony was interrupted before its completion by a mob of boys, and both patron and poet put to flight. One specimen of his laudatory verses may be seen on page 29 of this work, which will give the reader some idea of his qualifications for the office to which he was elected. How well he was satisfied with the praises of the poet we are not informed, but feeling probably that no person but himself could do justice to the ideas, which he wished to present to the public, he commenced writing for the press. Several of these effusions were printed in the newspapers.—The larger part of them written at different times are embodied in the present work, a large edition of which was published by himself and given away. In this edition not a stop or a mark was used in any line of his writings, but in the second edition one entire page was filled with stops and marks, with a recommendation from the author to his readers, to use them where they were wanted in the work, or in his own language, "to peper and soolt it as they pleased." Dexter had two children, Samuel and Nancy, neither of whom was distinguished for strength of intellect. The son was a dissipated prodigal and died young. The daughter, of whom mention is made by the father in the following pages, was married to Abraham Bishop of New Haven, who we are informed treated her with neglect and cruelty. A divorce followed and she became intemperate, lost what little reason she had, and is still living, a wretched object. Lord Dexter himself, if we may judge from his own writings and from what we have heard, was not happy in his domestic relations. He complains much of his wife, whom he calls the "gost," and charges the cause of his separation from her for thirteen years to his son Bishop. His own temper was irascible, and several stories are told of the excesses, into which it would sometimes lead him. He ordered his painter, Mr. Babson, to place the word "Constitution" on the scroll in the hand of the figure of Jefferson, which the latter, knowing the artist designed it to represent the Declaration of Independence, refused to do. Dexter was so incensed by this refusal, that he went into the house, and brought out a pistol, which he deliberately fired at the painter; but he was a poor shot, and the ball missing its object, entered the side of the house. At another time, seeing a countryman, as he thought, rather impudently viewing his premises, he ordered his son to fire at the stranger. He refused to do so, when the father threatened to shoot him unless he complied. His son then obeyed. The stranger escaped unhurt, but entered a complaint, and Lord Timothy was, in consequence, sentenced to the house of correction for several months. He went thither in [5]his own coach, priding himself on being the first man who had been to the county house in his own carriage, drawn by two splendid horses. He soon grew tired, however, of his confinement, and procured a release, which it was said, cost him a thousand dollars. The individual, who exercised most influence over Dexter was a negro woman, named Lucy Lancaster, or as she was commonly called "Black Luce," a woman of uncommon strength of mind, great shrewdness and remarkable for her powers of memory and knowledge of human nature, but as wicked as she was sagacious. She thought him an honest man, and not so deficient in intellect as many people supposed, and attributed his eccentricities to an excess of animal spirits.—This was probably to some extent true, though it is certain that other spirits contributed in no small degree to the excesses of his temper and the peculiarities of his taste. He was addicted to drunkenness, and with his son and other companions, kept up his revels in the best apartments of his house, by which in a very short time, all his costly furniture was ruined, or very much injured.

"Not insensible that he must share the common lot, Dexter, many years before his death, prepared himself a tomb. It was the basement story of his summer-house, magnificently fitted, and open to the light of day. His coffin, made of the best mahogany which he could find, superbly lined, and adorned with silver handles, he kept in a room of the house, and took great pleasure in exhibiting it to visitors—at other times it was locked up. Soon after his death apparatus was prepared, Dexter got up a mock funeral, which with all but his family and a few associates was to pass as real. Various people in the town were invited by card, who came and found the family clad in mourning, and preparations for the funeral going forward. The burial service was read by a wag, who then pronounced a bombastic eulogy upon the deceased. The mourners moved in procession to the tomb in the garden, the coffin was deposited, and they returned to the large hall, where a sumptuous entertainment was provided. While the feast was going on, a loud noise attracted the guests to the kitchen, where they beheld the arisen Lord caning his wife for not having shed a tear during the ceremony! He entered the hall with the astonished mourners, in high spirits, joined in the rout, threw money from the window to the crowd of boys, and expressed his satisfaction with every thing except the indifference of his wife, and the silence of the bells."

Lord Dexter died at his house, on the 26th of October, 1806, in his 60th year, and by direction of the

Board of Health, his remains were interred in the common burying place. His grave is marked by a simple stone.

The Dexter mansion, is yet standing, and is a very fine tenement, but retains few traces of the whims of its late proprietor. Of the images, upwards of forty in number, only the three Presidents now remain, the others having been cast down by the resistless hand of time. Some of them were blown down in the great gale of September, 1815, and were sold at auction.

The cut fronting the Biography gives a very excellent and faithful representation of Lord Dexter in his walking habits, and the likeness of the dog is equally perfect. The dog was perfectly black and the skin as entirely free from hair as that of an elephant. He differed as much from other dogs as did his master and his friend, the poet, differ from other people. The likenesses of all three were drawn with great accuracy by James Aiken, Esq. now a resident of Philadelphia, and could the patron and the poet be seen in proper person, dressed in the costume of that day, they would be objects of great curiosity. But they are gone, and of each it may be truly said, We ne'er shall look upon his like again.

View of Lord Dexter's Mansion, High Street,
Newburyport, 1806.

A PICKLE
FOR THE KNOWING ONES.

To mankind at Large the time is Com at Last the grat
day of Regoising what is that why I will tell you thous
three kings is Rased Rased you meane should know
Rased on the first Royal Arch in the world olmost Not
quite but very hiw up upon so thay are good mark to be
scene so the womans Lik to see the frount and all people
Loves to see them as the quakers will Com and peape
slyly and feele glad and say houe the doue frind father
Jorge washeton is in the senter king Addoms is at the

Rite hand the present king at the Left hand father gorge with his hat on the other hats of the middel king with his sword king Addoms with his Cane in a grand poster Adtetoude turning his fass towards the first king as if they was on sum politicks king our present king he is stands hearing being younger and very deafe in short being one grat felosfer Looks well East & west and North & south deafe & very deafe the god of Natur has dun very much for our present king and all our former ones they are all good I want them to Live for Ever and I beleave thay will it is hard work to be A king—I say it is hardar than tilling the ground I know it is for I find it is hard work to be A Lord I dont desier the sound but to pleas the peopel at Large Let it gou to brak the way it dus for Asort ment to help a good Lafe to Cour the sick spleney goutey dul frames Lik my selfe with the goute and so on make merry a Chealy Christen is for me only be onnest No matter what they worshep son moune or stars or there wife or miss if onnest Live forever [8]money wont gitt thous figers so fast as I wish I have sent to Leg horn for many mr bourr is one Amonks others I sent in the grand Crecham thous 3 kings Are plane white colow at present the Royal Arch & figers cost 39 pound wate silver the hiest Councaton order in the world so it is sade by the knowing one I have only 4 Lions & 1 Lam up the spred Eagel has bin up 3 years upon the Coupelay I have 13 billors front in strat Row for 13 states when we begun 3 in the Rear 15 foot hie 4 more on the grass see 2 the same hath at the Rite of the grand Arch 2 at the left wing 15 foot hie the Arch 17 foot hie the my hous is 3 sorey upwards of 290 feet round the hous Nater has formed the ground Eaquel to what you would wish for the Art by man Eaquel to a Solomun the onerabel Jonathan Jackson one of the first in this Country for tast borne A grat man by Nater then the best Lurning what sot me fored for my plan having so gran spot the hool of the world Cant Excead this to thous that dont know would think I was Like halfe the world A Lier I have traveled good deale but old steady men sayeth it is the first that it is the first best in this Contry & others Contrey I tell you this the trouth that None of you grat men wodent be A frunted at my preseadens & I spare Now Cost in the work I have the tempel of Reason in my garding 3 years past with a toume under it on the Eage of the grass see it cost 98 gineys besides the Coffen panted whit in side and out side tuched with green

Nobel trimings uncommon Lock so I can tak the kee in side and haye fier works in the toume pipes and tobacker & A speaking trumpet and & bibel to Read & sum good songs

What is a presedent answer A king bonne partey the grate has as much power as A king and ort to have & it is a massey he has for the good of mankind he has as much power as Any king for grat ways back there must be A head sum whare or the peopel is Lost Lik wild gees when thay Lous the gander two Leged want A head if fore Leged both & 2 Leged fouls the Name of presedent is to pleas the peopel at Large the sound souts best Now in the south give way to the North the North give way to the south or by & by you will brake what falers be wise on keep the Links to gether and if you cant A gree Consoalated to A kingly power for you must keep together at the wost hear it Labers ye les see there is so many men wants be the all offesers & Now sogers poor king Every day wants A bone sum more then others the king cant Live without the feald wee have had our turne grat good father Addoms [9]turne & turne About Rest Easey you all will be pleased with the present king give time all did I say Now but the magor part fore fifths at least.

TIMOTHY DEXTER

Frinds hear me 2 granadears goss up in 20 days fourder frinds I will tell the A tipe of man kind what is that 35 or 36 years gone A town caled Noubry all won the Younited states Noubry peopel kept to gether quiet till the Larned groed strong the farmers was 12 out of 20 thay wanted to have the offesers in the Contry the Eaned in the see port wanted to have them there geering A Rose groued warme fite thay wood in Law thay went the Jnrel Cort to be sot of finely thay go there Eands Answered the see port caled Newbury Port 600 Eakers of Land out of thirty thousand Eakers of good Land so much for mad peopel of Larning makes them mad if thay had kept to gether they wood have bin the sekent town in this stat A bout halfe of boston Now men mad to be in offess it hurts the peopel ot Large Like Carying the Innegent Lam to the slarter Now it would done to dewide the North from the south all won what I have Leade down but now keep to gether it is Like man and wife in troue Love Now guving death in the grander you will sous the glory I say keep to gether dont brak the Chane Renoue brotherle Love Never fade Like my box in my garding be one grat familey give way to one A Nother thous changes is the tide hie warter & Loue warte hie tids & Loue tids for my part I have Liked all the kings all three all our broken marchants cant have beaths of proffett gone and till the ground goue to work is all that has bin to Coleage goue with slipers and promis to pay and Never pay only with A Lye I gess 4 fifths is Coleage Lant or devel Lant or pretended to be onnest free masions but are to the Contrey for give me for gessing I hope it is Not so the Leaned is for Leovs & Littel fishes moses was but A man and Aaron thay had sum devel like my selfe man is the same give him power I say the Cloak Cukement maters the worst of cheats we hant got ony N Port wee are Noted to be the first in the North sabed Day is Not halfe A Nuf Night meatens it maks work for the Docters and Nuses Caaching Could but them Lives breed fast to mak up for them that dies poor creaters I pittey them so preast Riden it is wickard to leave poor sols in to the grave all our minesters are imported Very good men foull of Love of Crist I kep them A mit Amen at present.

The yong man that doth most all my Carving his work is much Liked by our grat men I felt founney one day I thort I would ask sade young man whare he was bone he sade Now whare what is all that Now whare was your mother over shaderd I says my mother was if I was to gess No I tell in Now town borne o on the water I says you beat me and so wee Lafed and it shuk of the spleane shoue him A Crows Neast he can carve one A fine fellow—I shold had all marbel if any bodey could to me the prise so I have sent for 8 busts for kings and grat men and 1 Lion & 2 gray hounds I hope to hear in foue Days to all onnest men

TIMOTHY DEXTER.

mister printter I must goue sum fourder I have got one good pen my fortin has bin hard very hard that is I have hard Noks on my head 4 difrent times from A boy to this Day twice taken up for dead two beating was a Lawyer then he was mad be Case the peopel at Large

Declared me Lord Dexter king of Chester this at my Contrey seet 26 mils from N Port my plase there is the fist from solt water to Canedy——this Lawyer that broused me was Judg Livermore son Arther the same Creater borid 200 dolors sum monts be fore this & then Oaded me he beat his bene factter it has bin my Luck to be yoused ten times wos by them I doue the most for I have Lost first and Last as much as A tun of silver grose my wife that was had 400 wut of silver Abraham bishup that married my dafter ten years gone him & shee sence then & my son Samuel L Dexter upwards of seventeene thousand Dolors the Rest by hamsher Col by Rougs has gokbey sekkent handed preasts Deakens gruntters whimers Every foue minnets A sith or Christ wee must be Leave in Crist o o Jeases will save us I thinks sum times the saving solt & smoak & solt peater will in time be very dear if it is yous the more smoak or the preasts will be out of work Littel Like fister france I Lade out A blan to have holerdays one Day in ten 24 years gone I thort it would save the Natision grat Deale of money sir in one sentrey then the preasts wood have time to studdery then hamer Down smartly make the sulffer smoak in their Nostils under the Cloak of bread & wine the hipecricks Cloven foots thay Doue it to get power to Lie and Not be mistruested all wars mostly by the suf the broken marchents are fond of war for thay hant Nothing to Lous & the minesters in all wars the Case o god Leave the Divel out when it is all Divel If you can [11]bare the trouth I will tell the trouth man is the best Annemel and the worst all men are more or less the Divel but there is sit of ods sum halfe sum three qurters the other part beast of Difrent kind of beasts sum one thing and sum a Nother sum Like a Dog sum Lik horses sum bare sum Cat sum Lion sum lik ouls sum a monkey sum wild Cat sum Lam sum A Dove sum a hogg sum a oxe sum a snake I want Desepons to be Dun A way but thay wont Never be as Long os prist Riden what Doue the preast prech to the Divel for all there hearaes old & youn more or Less the Divel I Liked to sade so Divel preaches to Divels Rebouking sin keep it up up up sayeth the hipacrits mockers of god habits an Costom is the ods ods maks the diffrence I sees god in all plases the god of Nater in all things wee Live and move in god he is the god of Nateer all Nater is god take one Ellement from us one of the fore take the fier or the water or or Eare or Earth wee are gone so wee Live in god Now Less us all be good children doue all things Rite the strong must bare the Infremiteys of the wicked shildren keep up tite Laws Draw the Ranes Littel harder stop theavs as fast as you can bad trade sheuuing Nine Numbers was Rot in 23 owers when I had hold of the pen five owers & 35 minnets A sort ment A sort ment is good in A shop———————

The preasts fixes there goods six days then thay open shop on sundays to sell there goods sum sets them of better than others bolerhed when a man is so week he wont doue for A Lawyer mak a preast of him for week thing to goue with week things the blind to Lead the blind so thay may fall into one Dich and so thay goue throue the world darkiness but foue peopel have A pinion of there one Not one in twenty as to this world goods and so it is as to the other world to Inquire the way goue to a fryer our peopel A bout the same thing only call it sumthing Else in Rum of a king call it president but preasts have money to save sols I want to know what a sole is I wish to see one Not a gizard I thinks the sole is the thinking part there is grat minds & Littel minds grat sols & Littel sols grat minds & littel minds According to the hevdey boddeys that has the power of our boddeys the same mother and the same father and six children how thay will differ in Looks complexions and axons sum for grat thing sum for littel things sumthing Nouw I say I say my figers will pay Intress money prove it first going over my brige sum more tole then helping the markett of the town Leeting hoses tavern keepers costom the honner to the town & my self.

TIMOTHY DEXTER.

one thing fourder I have bin convarted upwards 30 years quite Resined for the day the grat day I wish the preast Node as much as I think I doue there harts would Leap up to glory to be so Reader for the time of Rejoisng to goue to goue to be maried to what a fine widow with hur lamp bourning the Lamps trimed with glorey the shaking quickers after thay git convarted and there sins washed A way thay stay at home & Let theus goue unclene and so it is much so with me I stay at home praying for theavs and Rougs to be saved Day and Night praying for siners poour creaters my hous keeper is in the dark was then bad Crasey to be saved shee says shee has sind against the holey gost I have Asked her what is shee says it is sumthing but cant find out way sends for the preast coms what is the mater gost gost Dear sir & the minester makes a prayer the gost went of mostly not all part stayed behind shee has bin Crasey Ever sence the prest cant Lay the sepont houe many Nick Names three things have so sayeth the preacher Amen Amen see fath I du

---

Noue mister printer *sir* I was at Noue haven 7 years and seven monts past at commencent Degrees going on 40 boys was tuck degrees to doue good or Not good the ole man with the hat on told them to suddey houeman Nater & walk as A band of brothers from that day I thort that all thous that was baot up to Coleage the meaning was to git there Liveing out of the Labeer If the Coleages was to continer one sentrey & keep up the game recken the cost of All from there cradel to 22 years old all there fathers and gurd inands to Lay out one houndred years intress & intress upon intress atress gess at it & cast it see houe many houndred thousand millons of Dolors it would Com to to mad Rougs and theavs to plunder the Labering man that sweats to git his bread good common Laning is the best sum good books is best well under stoud be onnest dont be preast Riden it is a cheat all be onnest in all things Now feare Let this goue as you find it my way speling houe is the strangest man

T DEXTER

fourder mister for A minester to git the tone is a grat pint when I lived in hamsher one Noue Lit babstis babler sobed A way just fineshing his sermon he says o good Lord I hop you will consider [13]what foue hints I have given and I will cleare it up sum time hence I am much wore down now the wether being very worme to day Less bray & so went on fire fire & brimstone & grunting & fithing and tried to cry & snufel & blow the sconks horne & sum the old souls & yong fouls sot to crying I tuck my hat and went out houe mankind & women kind is imposed upon all over the world more or less by preast craft o for shame o for shame I pittey them

be onnest doue as you would wish others to doue unto
you in all things Now fear of Death Amen

T D'r

fourder what difrent wous wee have of this world &
the other world two good women Lived in A town
whare I once lived one was sick of a consumson Near
Death both belonged to the Church very onnest only
the well woman was week in wous & thing says unto the
sik woman I thinks you will see my housbon doue tell
him I and my son A greus very well and wee are all well
and the sow is piged and got seaven prittey pigs and fare
you well sister this I beleave is serting troue & so fare the
well—I shall com A gane in Littel while

and fourdermore I am for sum foue Decephons but
very foue fouer then Deathe preast craft is very good for
what to make old women gront and yong children cry
and old fouls fling snort o ye's and brak up farimeys
Doun by untrouths Lying and swaring to A Lye stop I
am a Live old me I have heard your wickard stuff you
have ingerd my frinds a plenty and if you dont stop I will

call forth one Abraham bishup to put Niklos and all that trys to keep up Lying if there should be any such stuf in the Land Church members pant to be fonnd of Desepchon thay are perfect but if there is any put them with the tufe bourne the Roubege pise on it or that feare Not wind or filth go by the Rackel breed and wos then tourd I Like to sade Now shite stink strong bread & wine master botill houe is the boull a black man a frind to John mekel jentel man from A Crows Nest Whare Now where ass Cole cole ass whare whare Now whare o yefs sum whare deare oilen Now the Ingons Lived there onle that Cant be he was from hell whare his or was brother came from oyes oyess o yess a Crows Neast or orgen pouler Down

FROM THE MUSEUM OF TIMOTHY DEXTER, ESQ.

Ime the first Lord in the younited States of A mercary Now of Newburyport it is the voise of the peopel and I cant Help it and so Let it goue Now as I must be Lord there will foler many more Lords prittey soune for it Dont hurt A Cat Nor the mouse Nor the son Nor the water Nor the Eare then goue on all in Easey Now bons broaken all is well all in Love Now I be gin to Lay the

Corner ston with grat Remembrence of my father Jorge Washington the grate herow 17 sentreys past before we found so good A father to his children and Now gone to Rest Now to shoue my Love to my father and grate Carieters I will shoue the world one of the grate Wonders of the world in 15 months if Now man mourders me in Dors or out Dors such A mouserum on Earth will annonce O Lord thou knowest to be troue fourder hear me good Lord I am A goueing to Let or shildren know Now to see good Lord what has bin in the world grat wase back to own fore fathers Not old plimeth but stop to Addom & Eve to shoue 45 figers two Leged and fore Leged becose we Cant Doue well without fore Legd in the first plase they are our foude in the Next plase to make out Dexters mouseum I wants 4 Lions to defend thous grat and mistry men from East to wist from North to South which Now are at the plases Rased the Lam is Not Readey in short meater if Agreabel I forme A good and peasabel govement on my Land in Newburyport Compleat I take 3 presedents hamsher govener all to Noue York and the grate mister John Jay is one, that maks 2 in that state the king of grat britton mister pitt Roufus King Cros over to france

Loues the 16 and then the grate bonnepartey the grate and there segnetoure Crow biddey—I Command pease and the gratest brotherly Love and Not fade be Linked to gether with that best of troue Love so as to govern all nasions on the fass of the gloub not to tiranize over them but to put them to order if any Despout shall A Rise as to boundreys or Any maturs of Importence it is Left france and grat britton and Amacarey to be setteled A Congress to be always in france all Despouts is to be thare seteled and this may be Dun this will balless powers and then all wars Dun A way there [15]fore I have the Lam to lay Dow with the Lion Now this may be Dun if thos three powers would A geray to Lay what is called Devel one side and Not Carry the gentelman pack hors Any longer but shake him off as dust on your feet and Laff at him there is a grate noise aboute a toue Leged Creter he says I am going to set sade black Divel there stop he would scare the womans so there would be No youse for the bilding I should have to E rect sum Noue won Now I stop hear I puts the Devil Long with the bull for he is a bulling 2 Leged Annemal stop put him one side Near Soloman Looking with Soloman to Ladey venus Now stop wind up there is grat ods in froute I will

Let you know the sekret houe you may see the Devel stand on your head before a Loucking glass and take a bibel in to your bousom fast 40 owers and look in the loucking glass there is no Devilif you dont see the ould fellow but I affirm you will see that ould Devel

Unto you all mankind Com to my hous to mock and sneare whi ye Dont you Lafe be fore god or I meane your betters think the heir power Dont know thorts and Axsions Now I will tell you good and bad it is Not pelite to Com to see what the bare walls keep of my ground if you are gentel men you would stay Away when all is Dun in marble I expect to goue out myself to Help if thous grat men will send on there Likeness all over the younited States I wish all the printers to give Notis if pleases to in form by printen in the Nouspapers for the good of the holl of man kind———

I waus to make my Enemys grin in time Lik A Cat over a hot puding and goue Away and hang there heads Doun Like a Dogg bin After sheep gilty stop see I am Afrade I Rite toue hash my peopel Complane of backker spittel maks work to Cleane it up——in the women skouls A bout it spit in ther hankershif or not spit A tall I must say sumthing or I should say Nothing therefore make sum Noise in the world when I git so ouely to Nash my goms and grising for water and that is salt water when brot A yong Devel to bring it and A Scoyer to wate and tend on gentelmen A black Suier his breth Smelt wos then bram stone by far but Let the Devel goue in to Darknes an takeld his due to Descare mankind for A Littel while this Cloven foot is seen be sum but the trap will over hall the Devel in tim I pittey this poore black man I thinc his master wants purging a Littel to har ber mr Devel A most but I did Not say Let him Run A way good Nit mr Devel Cary the sword and mwney with you tak John mekel Jentel man good Not

T DEXTER

THIS COMETH GREETING

mister printers the Igrent or the Nowing wons says I ort to Doue as thay doue to keep up Cheats or the same thing Desephons to Deseave the Igrent so wee may Cheat and Likewise have wars and plunder my wish is all Liers may have there part of fier and brimstone in this world or at least sum part of it or Else the gouement is Not good it will want pourging soone if A Lawyer is to way Lay a man and brouse him unmassely All most to Death A sitteson that pays twentey fore Dolors for Careags and not more then one Dolor A week to ment the hiways and my being Libperel is in part of this bloddey Afare No sauage would beat a man as I was beaten almost to Death I Did not know houe these men Came to keep sade Lawyer from quit killing of me till sum time After three men saw the Axon of the blodey seene without massey and carried sade Dexter in to the house sun fanting or Neare to se and behold the orful site bleading and blind of one Eye twoue brousings in two hours at Least Now Laws in this part of the world for A man of money to Live those I lend money to and A Lawyer and others thay youse me the wost it maks Inemys then these Rogs if there is Any that call me A soull and pick a Qualrel with me A bout my Nous papers so as to pay the Lawyer Craft to make up the molton Calf A molton Calfe Not an Ox Now the town of Chester has Lost two *Hundred wate of Siver* at Least I beleuv more money Now thay may have me in the town or A Lawyer Chouse for yourselves my frinds and felow mortels pease be with you All A men selagh finely brethren sum thing more Coming——

Chester, Sept. 29, 1796.

TIMOTHY DEXTER

For the Impartial Herald.

Messrs. Blunt & March,

I say to whom it may concern—to the majesty of the people of Newburyport, Greeting—

It costs Eight hundred Dollars a year to support a watch in this town, and yer gentlemen's windows are broken, fences pulled down and Cellars broken open, and much other misdemeanors done at night. Are the watch asleep, or are they afraid to detect those who are guilty of such practises? Boast not of it if you call this Liberty and Equality. Newburyport has had the name of being [17]a very civil worthy place; it is a great pity some bad boys or young men should disgrace it. I hope our worthy and honorable rulers will bring those rude lads to see themselves and lick the dust like serpents, and ask forgiveness of their betters, and do so no more, but repent and live.

Now fellow citizens is it wisdom, is it policy, to use a man or men so shocking bad as to oblige them to leave the town where they paid one Dollar a day to support government?

A friend to good order, honor to whom it belongs—to great men a friend—to all good citizens and honest men good bye.

Whereas many philosophers has judged or guessed at many things about this world, and so on. Now I suppose I may guess, as it is guessing times. I guess the world is one very large living creature, and always was, and always will be without any end from everlasting to everlasting, and no end. What grows on this large creature is trees and many other things. In the room of hair the rocks is moulds. This is called land where the hair grows, the belly the sea—all kinds of fish is the worms in the belly. This large body wants dressing to get our living of this creature and by industry we get a living—we and all the animal creation is less than fleas in comparison on the back or belly of this very large immense body. Among the hairs to work this great body is that of nature, past finding out.—All we know is we are here, we come into the world crying and go out groaning. Mankind is the master beast on the earth—in the sea, the whale is the head fish—the minim is the smallest fish—the great fish eat up the little ones, and so not only destroy one another, but they are master over the whole of beasts and fish, even over a lion, therefore man is the masterly beast and the worst of the whole— they know the most, and act the worst according to what they know. Seeing mankind so bad by nature, I think when the candle goes out, men and women is done, they will lay as dirt or rocks till the great gun fires, and when that goes off the gun will be so large that the gun will contain nine hundred million tons of the best of good powder, then that will shake and bring all the bones together, then the world will be to an end. All kinds of music will be going on, funding systems will be laid aside, [18]the melody will be very great. Now why cant you all believe the above written as well as many other things to be true; as well as what was set forth in the last Centinel concerning digging up a frog twenty five feet below the surface, where it was most as hard as a rock—there was his shape like taking a stone out of a rock—This is from a minister. Now why wont you believe me as well.

WONDER OF WONDERS!

How great the soul is! Do not you all wonder & admire to see and behold and hear? Can you all believe half the truth, and admire to hear the wonders how great the soul is—only behold—past finding out! Only see how large the soul is!—that if a man is drowned in the sea, what a great bubble comes up out of the top of the water! the last of the man dying under water—this is wind—is the soul that is the last to ascend out of the deep to glory—it is the breath from on high doth go on high to glory. The bubble is the soul. A young fellow's for gunning for the good of bodies and souls.

My frinds & felow mortals there is A first Cose of all things most Comle so it Came to pass that one Abraham bish up got A qanted with my Dafter—shee A babey he Old in Eage and Larning and Colage Lant & Lawyer Lant and preast Lant and masonik Lant and Divel Lant he was then Nothing as for Cash he being A fox and A old fox he was After the graps he tasted of them he Cryed out fower this Anne meal sent my Dafter home he sad A b did Not git all the Lovs & Littel fishes but got A part and Now 9 years I have Now had my Dafter Crasey in & by the Cose of this wild A & b hell on Earth o o pittey me All good felow mortels sade Creater A b mad with Larning & as pour as A snake and as proud as Lousfer he sade his father was worth twenty thosand Dolors & he was Not more than five thousand Dolors he send for bishup bass to be mared befor dublessed & Insisted to be maried he says Daxter may Crye them Down in the Lore Reogon After sum time thay got published then he in sisted Not to have Any witness went and [19]hid finly my gost my wife that was the gost 13 yearst Last march thay where maried I was maried to the gost thirtey five Last may I have bin in hell all the time more so sence Abraham bishup got in to my house he hurt me and familey one tun of silver it was the Cose of my parting with mis Dexter Now I Am free Now for A wife that has A sole the gost was A gisard & A Cose all Round her A b striking my Dafter on hur side as shee swares to grat Lawyer Dexter and to many others I be Leave it that knows the trouth the bloue he gave hur on the side shee had to put plasters on her side Neare three years when Likker is in the wit is scattered A b is the beast or Creater two Leged Conekett boull short Nek boull head thik hare big sholders black Corlley hare he wants to be A god but what I sot sade Creater Down at short A quatence I Can prove it my selfe by men of the sekent magentoude my gesing of the Creater it tourned out According to my gessing and when I see my father the grat good man father Thomas gefsion I will Let the

Cat out of the bag and give Lite to the blind sade A b will Doue for sum offess Everye Annemel will Doue for sumthing A b will mak a midling good CAMP COLLEMON A thing hier if I am a Roug in grane so be it A Lepard Cant Alter hur spots Nor beaver wont groue on A houk back I be Leave if my father the presente koue the holl trouth of A b treatment to my Dafter from her mouth the grat man woul shead tears with greafe and all good peopel Like wise shocking is the A fare

I am

TIMOTHY DEXTER

To man kind at Large I Never had the honour to be Long I meane to that onerabel mesonek Order I Noked once once twise three times & the gohst Apeared sade thou shall Not enter be Cose I have toue much knowledge in my head—I sopose had I bin one then should bin to keep open Dors for thives & Robers I have Rougs plentey without keeping tavern I Dont wont Now Abrahams Nor Aney of the order only fict Ladeys mared and grat gentil men that belongs out of the town mared peopol and fine widders I wish to see with pleasur for I wonts to marey A fine wider for I hant had Now wife for thirteene years Next orgest I gave the gost fore hundred wate of silver to quit the state grat Lawyer passons the gient of the Law Rote the Contract the Cose of it was that mis [20]Dexter that was would have my Dafter marey to A bishup Cosed the A greement the sole Cose she has two trousteays which have the money to deal out the intress and shee is so ginress shee bys hur Neadels I bys the pins & sisers & all things Else shee Leaves the in tress in the hands of the trosteys I must have A Companon soun good by all At present with glorey

TIMOTHY DEXTER

I ask for giveness of the world of mankind for teling the trouth I meane No hurt to A flie only when he bits me then I kils the flye if I can I have bin my one tromter fore teene years my tromter is Dead my haveing so many wounds in fas and on my head I Doue it to make a good Lafe to keep my sperets from sinking pittey me all good peopel A men

and fourder I maried widder frothingham shee had fore Children the holl of all there stats was short of thirteene houndred Dolors this woman groed mad shee sade shee must goue to hell goue ferting for I have fined A ganst the holey goast un pardinbell sin shee was for making way with hur selfe in three monts I got the best minister in town to Lay the gost he prayed hartey but Could Not Laye the serpent only in part shee has bin Cracey Every sence it is A wonder I am A Live two children suked hur brest—it is heretarey two Children maried now Live upon me being disorded thay beat me offen with Death Cloube & the old gost toue bad to say I be silent under serkoumstanes I mus Cout & Roum sell the one of the first plases all most in the world for I am in grat fear of my Life being taken A way such blows I have had from toue or three gost in my familey is worth twelve hundred hoxets of geamator best shougers Even A saxton to take the blows I wodent for fifty milon Dollors words cant Express the bloddey war in my

familey three gosts all Noys Robing of me I must sell
with tears in my Eys I Cant see to Rite Aany more fare
well I say good bye

T DEXTER

How Did Dexter make his money Inw ye says bying
whale bone for stain for ships in grosing three houndred
& 40 tuns bort all in boston salum and all in Noue york
under Cover oppenly told them for my ships thay all
Lafed so I had at my one prise I had four Couning men
for Rouners thay souned the horne as I told them to Act

the fool I was foull of Cash I had Nine tun of silver on hand at that time all that time the Creaters more or Less Lafing it spread very fast heare is the Rub in fifty Days thay smelt A Rat found whare it was gone to Nouebry Port speklaters swarmed Like hell houns to be short with it I made seventey five per sent one tun and halfe of silver and over one more spect Drole A Nouf I Dreamed of warming pans three Nits that thay would doue in the west ingas I got not more than fortey two thousand put them in Nine vessele for difrent ports that tuck good hold———I cleared sevinty nine per sent———the pans thay mad yous of them for Coucking very good master for Coukey blessed good in Deade missey got Nise handed Now bourn my fase the best thing I Ever see in borne days I found I was very luckkey in spekkelasion I Dreamed that the good book was Run Down in this Countrey Nine years gone so Low az halfe prise and Dull at that the bibbel I means I had the Readey Cash by holl sale I bort twelve per sent under halfe prise thay Cost forty one sents Each bibels twenty one thousand I put them into twenty one vessels for the westinges and sent A text that all of them must have one bibel in Every familey or if not thay would goue to hell and if thay had Dun wiked flie to the bibel and on thare Neas and kiss the bibel three times and Look up to heaven Annest for giveness my Capttens all had Compleat orders heare Coms the good Luck I made one hundred per sent & Littel over then I found I had made money A Nuf I hant speck A Lated sence old times by goverment secourties I made or cleared forty seven thousands Dolors that is the old A fare Now I toald the all the sekrett Now be still Let me A Lone Dont wonder Now more houe I got my money boaz

T DEXTER

Now to all onnest men to pittey me that I have bin in hell: 35 years in this world with the gost A woman I maried and have two Children Now Liveing Abram bishup mared my Dafter sence the troubel is such that words Cant be Exprexed Nine years disorded [22]for a tun of silver for three months I could Not have the gost in my pallas sleep Not have to be had Now to save my

Life I will sell if Not I will Let the house it is as Notted as Any hous in the oile shouls and furder in the world or sence Noers Arke & sence the floud taking in my self finly such A plase No whare in the world all gous with it hoses chareags all but plate & gouels A Reserve the holey bybel and one bouck more my old head has wore out three boddeys it would take a journey of Docters one our to find and Count the scars on my head given by the goust & others Amen

Joune 12- 1805 Clean trouth

T DEXTER

I say the grate mister Divel that has so maney Nick Names a frind to the preasts Now is dead all and the pope Likewise and the founders of mesonic A Cheat foull of war and gratness of hell Dead preasts Dead and Lawyers Damede Deade A braham b bi Ass Dead and All the frinds of mankind sings prasses that wee are the grat familey of mankind Now out of hell Deleured from fire and smoak bourning for Ever Now all in heaven uppon Earth Now all frinds Now for A Day of Regoising all over the world as one grate familey all Nasions to be ounited No more wars for fifty years and Longer I Recommend pease A Congress in france and when wee are Ripe for A Emper in this Contrey Call for me to take the helm or a Consler in the Afare of trouth Amen and Amen

TIMOTHY DEXTER

P S—one thing further I happened not to think of that grate Creature which some fools Call the Goast and others say that he is wanted—But I thing that it will be of searvice to let the Thanttron Dye

T DEXTER

Scarting trouths fortey six years gone old french war to git men and Lads to List the prests told them thay would Live as Long as if thay staed at home for Every boulitt had its Commison from the Lord he directed them one time when old good mister Emmerson had A gurnemon to preach I heard him say for Addom sin there was Now in hell milons of milons of Children Not more than A [23]span Long all this is troue and when there was a A Drouth most over thay would Call A fast and pray very Annest for the bottels of heaven to be on Corked so the Rane mit Com Down the minester did Not say how Larg thay whare I gess they held five hundred hoxetts Each

1805 may 27

TIMOTHY DEXTER

Trouth I afirme I am so much of A foule the Rougs want to git my Jouels & Loavs & Littel fishes without my Leave Leave is Lit thay all Caled me A foull forty years Now I will Call all fouls but onnes men Now to brove me A foull I Never Could sing Nor play Cards Nor Dance Nor tell A Long storey Nor play on Any mouskel Nor pray Nor make A pen when I was young I Could play on A Jous harp it would mak my mouth warter and the Ladeys sumthing warter gess what I sade Nothing A good Lafe is beter than Crying A Clam will Cry And warter wen thay are out of there Ellemen so wee the same if I had Not the gost in my house I would I mean give Lite to my brothers & sisters and have A pease all over the world and beat the trouthe into my frinds houe goud it is houe onnest it would be and houe man kind has bin in posed upon & houe thay have bin blinded with untrouths gosts and mister Divels there is Now None of that order all Lye the mesonek if thay wilt make a book of trouth I will give the Creaters but I will take the Chare and put my frind bonne partey on my Rte hand And the grat ginrel meroue on my Left hand A Nuf to give the sword is in the banks A Emper only be still I will take the helm in Love I am A quaker No blod spiled all in the Love of A Emper you will have in fortey years I may Com back & see houe you all goue on & what you ware when the gost is gone and mister Divel pease on Earth be fore I will have a war in my Day I will be your frind the Emper and if I want help I will Call my frind boneypartey and gorge the third & Dewide the Lose Now take Care peas I say Except of what is Rewealed to me for it will Com to pass I was born when grat powers Rouled I was borne in 1747 Janeuarey 22 on this day in the morning A grat snow storme the sines in the seventh house wives mars Came fored Joupeter stud by houlding the Candel I was to be one grat man mars got the beth to be onnest man to Doue good to my felow mortelz I think I am A quaker [24]but I have so Littel sense I Cant Deseave I Can swep my hous & git all A Noue gelt & goue out of hell is bless Law and trouth and Reason on my side it must be done when I git my worthy widdow it is Dun Not one word of Anger as Long as I Live to a A good woman I a firme

TIMOTHY DEXTER

fourder I Dont have Aney of the Ladeys of prinsbell spend the Intress I will spend Day and Nite All I have and Doue all the good to please I can make as much heaven upon Earth as posbel and then Dye in peas A men and Amen for A Companon I must have to make out this heaven then I am happy the goue in the dark in pease when the Candel gous out in the—Lord god of Nater one more A men good bye

T DEXTER

forder A grate good man Came to see me Not Long sence I told sade man I had many Innemys he says be Cos you are toue onnest to be beloved you Dont gine in Comon ways with Rougs bibel making mesonik order to promes to pay & Never pay only with A Lye and gine heell on Earth Cheat all you Can gine the mob then you are A brother Now I am glad I did Not Nock the Doer Down my good Louck my god and my god blessed be my good Luch

T DEXTER

sum more sweet meats & trouths I say Now man sence Noers Ark Dare to Rite of so Littel Laning I begon when abrham was in my hous I then Rote this world was hell & men was Divels sum better then others sum white Divels sum black & sum Copper Divels I for got them bloue Divels this spred far was printed in many papers a bishop Cosed my blood to bile thirteene years last March as when I begun to Rite I sade the grat Rougs was the best men o o for shame the onnest man was Lafed at & a b being foull of Larning it maks him mad to be a Lousefer his Rane is short I hope to see my father the grat felosfer the presedent before I die the trouth he must know a men

TDEXTER

I Crys Crys Lik a babey when I Rits my trobel is so grat to have my Dafter so Crasey the Rick of our Lives such blows with such weapons of a sudden & strike such brouses is worth thirty [25] millon of Dolors for a pouer man to have and others o brous me thay wont my Life to git my money & so I must seel & be a sitteson of the world it is a wonder I am a Live the burds will Chip offen before I Can git to sleep the Noys is so grate all hell No more a b bishups he wants to be Deatey Let sade beast goue once & twise act so Now toue much Laning make Rougs and fouls in the Eand Dig a Dich & fall in to it white Rop or a hare Rop taks them in time

trouth

This is revealed to me how the world was made with what stuff it was made with is the question Now I tell the with paper pen and ink and type the Anemels to be the founders of it with a Lye & Lyes upon Lyes wose then beasts or Snaks or wouls or bars tigers Divils and ten times wose with all Lyes untrouths the world allways was and is Look out for trouth a men I

TIMOTHY DEXTER

fourder in six Days and verey good and harde Laber I Cant gitt my monement Dun in sixty Days and work hard very hard & sweet it was for want of maney hands I had No hiram Nor Solomon only my selfe

T DEXTER

World makers mankind with marbel and parchment and paper pen & ink and printers tips and Lyes upon

Lyes amen and amen the world was made in six Days out of Nothing o yess o lye Now all troue Lye yess all the world over

TIMOTHY DEXTER

APPENDIX.

IN HONOR OF
TIMOTHY DEXTER, ESQ.

This great philosopher may indeed be styled a phenomenon in nature! The many literary qualifications he possesses rank him foremost among literary characters.——That unequalled production from the pen of this wonderful philosopher, denominated *"A Pickle for the Knowing Ones,"* has not only received universal applause, and been ranked as of the first magnitude in the literary world, but has had such rapidity in its sale, that a copy cannot be procured, though diligently sought after by men of the most transcendant merit.

Where can we find a man so extensively useful, and so eminently calculated to diffuse light to a dark and ignorant multitude, as this rare philosopher? How penetrating his understanding! How deep his ideas! What a multitude of discoveries which before were hid in embryo, have made their appearance at the nod of his genius! Surely we may say, Blessed are the people who are highly favored with the greatest Luminary that ever gave light to an existing world!!

While aiming at a just portrait of this remarkable Naturalist and Philosopher, his generosity is no less a subject of admiration, than his literary and philosophical abilities. The readiness with which his benevolent soul bestows donations calls forth the grateful acknowledgement of all who have been liberally assisted from his bountiful hand.

See him the first to assist in building a church for the worship of God! See him liberally give for the purchase of bells, the ready cash, without hesitation! See him expending his fortune to preserve in everlasting romembrance, characters who have shone with [27]unexampled greatness in Europe and America!

Here the subject fails. Vain man may as well attempt to stop the course of nature, as to do ample justice to this wonderful man!

> Behold all nature stands aghast
> To hear thy fame from east to west!
> How great how grand of thee we hear,
> Thou man of sense—thou eastern star!
> All men inquire—but few can tell
> How thou in science doth excel!
> Great philosophic genius, we,
> The meanest reptiles, bow the knee.
> At thy majestic shrine we shrink!
> What can we do, or say, or think!
> When contemplating on thy worth.
> Which hath astonish'd all the earth.
> Great DEXTER, did the world do right,
> Thy name would shine with brilliant light!
> Each would declare thy wond'rous fame,
> And shout at DEXTER'S mighty name!

Salem, *June 14, 1805*

My Lord Dexter,

By the politeness of Mr. *Emerson* I received the very valuable contents of your package. A new edition of that unprecedented performance, entitled "A Pickle for the Knowing Ones," &c. is very urgently called for by the friends of literature in this country and in England—and I presume with the additions and improvements intended to accompany the second edition, provided it should be well printed, would entitle the author to a seat with the Disciples of Sir Joseph Banks, if not to a place in Bonaparte's Legion of Honor—for my Lord DEXTER is an honorable man. But, sir, the work cannot be executed for the sum named—nor in the time specified.—I will print an edition of 500 copies with the additions, for fifty dollars, and cannot possibly do them for less.

Wishing your Lordship health in perpetuity—a continuance of your admirable reasoning faculties—good *spirits*, and an abundance of wealth—and finally a safe passage over any river not with *Sticks*, but a pleasure boat, I remain yours with the utmost profundity.

W. CARLTON.

The   Right   Honorable   Lord Dexter, *Kt. Newburyport.*

The follering peases are not my Riting but very drole

TIMOTHY DEXTER

Mr. Melcher,

> *Your publishing the following extract from a letter said to be from a trader among the Indians to a friend, may amuse some of your customers for the Gazette.*

A few days ago one of the Indians paid me a visit. After some conversation, he said that a minister from the United States had been with his tribe to teach them the Christian religion. He says that there is but one only living and true God, who is a good, wise, and powerful spirit (this Indian say too) and that there are three persons in the god head, of one substance and power, God the father, God the Son and God the Holy Ghost, that the Father is of none, neither begotten, or proceeding, the Son is eternally begotten of the Father, the Holy Ghost eternally proceeding from the Father and the Son, and that the Holy Ghost visited a virgin, and conveyed the Son into her; where he continued nine moons and then was born like other children, was born God and man, that when he was about thirty years old began to preach, but the great men no like his preaching, sent their warriors, who took and killed him.

Indians ask what all this talk mean, he say that the first man and woman broke God's law in eating what God had forbidden, that therefore they and all the children that should proceed from them must die, and be punished after death forever; that the Son came and died to save some of mankind from being punished after death. Oh! 'trange that man could kill God the Son, and that his death be of service to mankind—great many people die before the Son of God, and did not know any thing about him—it was then asked whether his dying would do poor Indians any good; he say yes, if they believe; then me say that pappoose no believe them do no good; he say you must leave that with God, and believe for yourself—one say it is hard to believe such 'tories; if Indian tell such 'trange things, the white people no believe um.

A curious Sermon, by the Rev. Mr. Hyberdin, which he made at the request of certain thieves that robbed him on a hill near Hartlgrow, in Hampshire, (England) in their presence and at that instant.

I greatly marvel that any man will disgrace thieving, and think that the doers thereof are worthy of death, considering it as a thing that cometh near unto virtue, being used in all countries, and allowed by God himself; the thing which I cannot compendiously show unto you at so short a warning, and on so sharp an occasion. I must desire you, gentle audience of thieves, to take in good part what at this time cometh into my mind, not doubting but that you, through your good knowledge, are able to add much more unto it, than this which I shall now offer unto you.

First, Fortitude and stoutness of courage, and also boldness of mind, is commended of some men to be a virtue; which being granted, who is there then that will not judge thieves to be virtuous? For they are of all men the most stout and hardy, and the most void of fear; for thieving is a thing usual among all men; for not only you that are here present, but also many others in divers places, both men, women and children, rich and poor, are daily of the faculty, as the hangman at Newgate can testify; and that it is allowed of by God himself is evident from Scripture; For if you examine the whole course of the Bible you will find that thieves have been beloved of God; for Jacob, when he came out of Mesopotamia, did steal his uncle Laban's kids. The same Jacob did also steal his brother Esau's blessing; and yet God said, *I have chosen Jacob and refused Esau.* The children of Israel, when they came out of Egypt, did steal the Egyptian's jewels of silver and jewels of gold, as God commanded them to do.

David, in the days of Abiathar, the high priest, came into the temple and stole the hallowed bread; and yet God said, "David is a man after my own heart." Christ himself, when he was here on earth, did take an ass and colt that was none of his; and yet God said, "This is my beloved son, in whom I am well pleased." *Thus you see that God delighted in thieves.*

But most of all I marvel that men can despise thieves, whereas in many points you be like Christ himself; for Christ had no dwelling place no more than you—Christ at length was caught, and so will you—he went to hell and so will you. In this you differ from him, for he rose and went into heaven—so you will [30]never do without God's great mercy, which God grant you. To whom with the Father, Son and Holy Ghost, be all honor and glory, for ever and ever. Amen.

From the Providence Phœnix of December, 1804.

MARQUIS OF NEWBURYPORT!!

[On Monday last arrived in this town the most noble and illustrious Lord TIMOTHY DEXTER, of Newburyport, Massachusetts, who

has since his arrival requested the publication of the following stanzas in this day's paper, as a humble tribute to the incomprehensible majesty of his name! While they serve as a brilliant specimen of the gifted talents and admirable sublimity of the Laureat, from whose pen they flowed, the virtuoso in genealogies, and the worshippers of noble rank and boundless fortune may derive a rich and delicious satisfaction from the subject to which they are devoted!

ADVERTISEMENT EXTRA.
OF THE CELEBRATED
LORD DEXTER.

LORD DEXTER is a man of fame,
Most celebrated is his name;
More precious far than gold that's pure,
Lord Dexter live for evermore.
His noble house it shines more bright
Than Lebanon's most pleasant height,
Never was one who step'd therein
Who wanted to come out again.
His house is fill'd with sweet perfumes,
Rich furniture doth fill his rooms;

Inside and out it is adorn'd,
And on the top an eagle's form'd.
His house is white and trimm'd with green,
For many miles it may be seen;
It shines as bright as any star,
The fame of it has spread afar.

[31]

Lord Dexter, thou, whose name alone
Shines brighter than king George's throne;
Thy name shall stand in books of fame,
And Princes shall his name proclaim.
Lord Dexter hath a coach beside,
In pomp and splendor he doth ride;
The horses champ the silver bitt,
And throw the foam around their feet.
The images around him stand,
For they were made by his command;
Looking to see Lord Dexter come,
With fixed eyes they see him home.
Four lions stand to guard the door,
With their mouths open to devour
All enemies who do disturb
Lord Dexter or his shady grove.
Lord Dexter, like king Solomon,
Hath gold and silver by the ton,
And bells to churches he hath given,

To worship the great king of heaven.

His mighty deeds they are so great,

He's honor'd both by church and state,

And when he comes all must give way,

To let Lord Dexter bear the sway.

When Dexter dies all things shall droop,

Lord East, Lord West, Lord North shall stoop,

And then Lord South with pomp shall come,

And bear his body to the tomb.

His tomb most charming to behold,

A thousand sweets it doth unfold;

When Dexter dies shall willows weep,

And mourning friends shall fill the street.

May Washington immortal stand,

May Jefferson by God's command

Support the right of all mankind,

John Adams not a whit behind.

America with all your host,

Lord Dexter in a bumper toast;

May he enjoy his life in peace,

And when he's dead his name not cease.

In heaven may he always reign,

For there's no sorrow, sin, nor pain:

Unto the world I leave the rest,

For to pronounce Lord Dexter blest.

Transcriber's Note: The block of punctuation (on a page by itself) is inexplicably left unexplained in this edition. Dexter wrote before it in the second edition:

"fouder mister printer the Nowing ones complane of my book the fust edition had no stops I put in A Nuf here and thay may peper and solt it as they plese"

The End

More books by Stefan James Madison coming soon!